Storytelling for Beginners:

The success factor in marketing

How to tell your story and turn customers into fans - incl. editorial plan checklist for the right content and 11-step action plan

Nicole Menrath

CONTENT

What you can expect in this guide

You've probably already realized that storytelling is ubiquitous today and that it's hard to imagine marketing without it. In this guide, you will first get an overview of what storytelling actually is and why it is an important part of a successful marketing strategy. In addition, you will learn in the theory section how a classic story is structured, to what extent this structure can be integrated into business practice and what alternatives there are. This again with the help of the probably best-known example of entrepreneurial storytelling - do you already guess which company we are talking about?

In a second, practice-oriented part, I will introduce you to storytelling step by step - from goal formulation and idea generation to editorial planning and the actual writing process to the target group- and platform-optimized publication of your story. You will learn why you need to define your goals and target groups precisely and why good planning is already half the battle. You'll see that storytelling goes far beyond the formulation of clumsy advertising slogans - and yet is just as far from a mindless enumeration of fact-based sales arguments. That is why the guidebook also contains a whole series of tips on "good writing". The topic of "monitoring and success control" will also be briefly touched on in the conclusion. Both within the individual chapters of the practical section and afterwards, you will find helpful checklists as well as various tips and tricks that will make your work easier in the long term.

For impatient or advanced readers, the practical section is followed by an 11-point quick guide that conveys in short form what I explained to you in detail earlier in the guide. Namely, how you can

rock your storytelling in marketing - and bring y-
our story from the planning to the publication and
subsequent success control structured unerringly
to the man (or woman).

Storytelling as a success factor in marketing

Nowadays, so-called storytelling is ubiquitous, especially in professions that have "something to do with media". That's why companies in general and their marketing departments in particular can no longer ignore it. Before you learn how you can use the power of storytelling for your marketing strategies, I would like to explain what storytelling is, why you can use it to stand out from your competitors and how you can gain better access to your customers.

WHAT IS STORYTELLING?

Storytelling is a type of infotainment based on the idea of convincing customers not through facts and figures (ZDF), but by building an emotional bond - or, to put it more simply: by telling stories. It derives from the English "story" and "to tell" and shows that some things never go out of fashion: people love stories. Most of all those that touch them emotionally. It doesn't matter whether it's a fairy tale, a fable or a Hollywood movie. What they all have in common is that the audience can identify with the hero and empathize with him. Just as stories have always been used to pass on complex knowledge in a comprehensible way, you can still use them today, for example, to specifically communicate the values of your company or to convince customers of the uniqueness of your products and services.

The (classic) structure of a story
Maybe you still darkly remember the time in German class when you asked yourself, "Why on earth do I need to know the five acts of a drama and their function?" Well, now you know: because storytelling is now an important way to beat the

competition, even in business. And because stories, in order to captivate the reader, need an arc of suspense.

Therefore, once again briefly and concisely: In the first act, the W-questions are answered, for example, Who? What? Where? And when? The initial situation is described, as is the (historical) context. Finally, the conflict begins to unfold, and in the second act it becomes more and more acute, finally reaching its climax in the third act: Will the hero triumph or will he fail? The penultimate act is followed by the so-called "retarding moment," i.e., an unexpected twist that delays the outcome of the conflict, and finally the (hopefully positive) resolution of the story/problem follows.

Stories in the corporate sector
Now you might throw your hands up in horror and ask yourself what this has to do with marketing and your company. And indeed, the classic structure is not suitable for every format of storytelling, as you will see in the practical part. Still, it's important to keep the structure in mind. After all, according to Simon Sinek, a company's storytelling should also focus on and answer at least

the following questions: *Why? How? And What?"* - with the main focus being on the "Why?". He calls this the **"Golden Circle,"** which answers the customer's most important questions about why they should choose you.

The lowest common denominator between normal stories and entrepreneurial storytelling lies in three components that every story, no matter how small or short, needs: Characters, a conflict and its resolution. This form of storytelling is therefore particularly suitable for your "About Us" page, your own blog or for product launches (see below).

WHY YOUR MARKETING BE-NEFITS FROM STORYTELLING

If you consider these outline characteristics, you will notice that a storytelling marketing text no longer has too much to do with a classic advertising text. But why should you bother? Many studies have shown that in times of the Internet and the accompanying flood of information, life is not only moving faster, but at the same time the human attention span is also becoming shorter. With all the stimuli constantly flowing at people, there is often no time or no desire to deal with a (complex) topic for longer than necessary. At the same time, consumers are becoming increasingly indifferent to purely factual information and clumsy advertising slogans due to the variety of sometimes almost identical products. Stories, on the other hand, generate attention because the listener can (ideally) identify with the narrator/hero.

Through this build-up of emotions, (implicit) conclusions are also drawn about the company and anchored in the memory accordingly. And this is precisely why storytelling is such an effective method for positively differentiating oneself from competitors. On the one hand, more complex facts can be better packaged, similar to the "moral of the story" found in Wilhelm Busch. On the other hand, you bind your customers to you with the help of emotions by showing them why your products and services are best suited to them and their needs through clever, funny or instructive stories.

Example from corporate practice: Apple

You don't believe that this is possible? Even though you may not have been aware of it, you are probably familiar with the most famous example of successful storytelling in corporate practice: that of Steve Jobs and Apple. Steve Jobs, the CEO of the tech company at the time, knew how to put Apple and its products in the best light like hardly anyone else. Not only because he himself was a charismatic speaker. But also because he managed to cleverly convey new products with the help of "tangible images" instead of simply rattling off numbers, data and facts to praise the merits of his products. And he did it consistently, from the product launch to the last detail of the advertising campaigns. Don't believe me? Well, then maybe you should take a look at the presentation of the iPod ("1000 songs in your pocket") or the first iPhone. Not only is a conflict presented there (for example, the impractical size of the Discmans and first MP3 players of the time), but also an antagonist (in the form of allusions to the "outdated" products of other manufacturers), which makes the hero (Apple's product, where a solution to the aforementioned conflict was found) look even better in direct comparison.

Apple is also a good example in terms of corporate history, because the company also conveys the "American way of life", i.e. the "from rags to riches" principle: two young men with a passion for computers and technology start out in a garage to develop a computer that is small and cheap enough that private individuals can also afford one. Finally, the user interface is to be developed in such a way that even people who are not familiar with program commands can use the computer intuitively. And so the product range gradually expands as soon as Steve Jobs in particular, who himself was also partly an artist and very attached to music, discovered possibilities for improvement in already existing technical products. The result is a company that is known worldwide in the field of consumer electronics and whose brand is so strong that the emotions associated with it alone are to a large extent enough to continue to secure the company large market shares.

To briefly come back to the "Golden Circle" at this point: Apple's why can probably best be summarized as "so that as many households/people as possible are able to afford the corresponding products and because there are still many possibilities for optimization". This also leads to the how: making computers (and later other technical products) smaller, more practical and, above all, more user-friendly. And finally, the what: Apple probes the market, looks at existing conflicts and seeks an innovative solution to be better/faster than the competition.

Using Apple as an example, you can gain even more insights in terms of corporate storytelling - for example, about what can be understood by a story, story or narrative. This in turn is important for your subsequent editorial planning. Because in addition to the classic structure of a story already mentioned above, storytelling in marketing encompasses a much broader range of formats. Starting with in-depth blog posts, which may well resemble a classic hero's journey in some circumstances, to presentations for product launches, to short stories in the form of captions on Instagram or individual tweets. And in addition to the more text-heavy formats, there is of course, depending on the platform, the option to switch to image-, sound- or video-based posts.

As you can see, you have almost unlimited possibilities to incorporate storytelling into your marketing strategies. The important thing is that you manage to offer the audience added value. And that you place your chosen hero, a conflict, and its resolution at the center of your narrative - thus ensuring that familiar images and emotions are aroused in your target group, which they will then in turn associate with you and your company.

In the following practical part of the guide, you will learn how to develop a storytelling strategy, implement individual articles, and then measure their success. In the process, you will discover that the preparatory work often requires more effort and time than the actual writing. True to the motto: good planning is half the battle. The main thing will be to find out exactly what your goal is, who your target group is and how best to reach them, but also how to generate and organize ideas - and what else you should pay attention to when writing.

How to tell your story(s)

In the first, more theory-heavy part of this guide, you learned that storytelling is important in marketing to positively stand out from the competition and to retain customers in the long term. You also learned that stories help people remember (complex) facts better. In addition, they need at least one hero, a conflict and its resolution, and a very visual presentation (in the literal or figurative sense) to captivate the addressee.

DEFINE GOALS AND FIND IDEAS

Before you start writing wildly, you should first take a close look at what goal you are pursuing with your storytelling and what story(s) you should tell so that you achieve exactly what you have set out to do. To do this, it can be useful to start by answering the so-called W-questions, similar to the way you used to do a school essay in German. As soon as these questions have been clarified, the identified goals should be formulated in such concrete terms that it is possible to monitor progress and success accordingly. You will also find more information on this later.

Checklist: The W questions as the most important basis
To get a clearer picture of which stories are positively influencing your marketing, especially the so-called content marketing, on your own channels at , you should first take enough time to answer the following questions as precisely as possible:

- **Why? What for?** This is about the goal pursued, i.e. the intention you have in publishing your story. Do you want to make the company better known? Individual employees? New products? Do you want to expand your customer service by answering frequently asked questions, for example? Do you want to recruit new employees or acquire new customers and investors?

- **Who is my target audience?** The more accurate the picture of the group of people you want to reach, the better you can tailor your story/s and the higher their chances of success. Try to be as specific as possible about who you want to target. Think about demographic and sociological characteristics, such as age, gender, social class/occupation/income, place of residence, health condition, personality type, interests ... and then ask yourself the question: what information and what kind of approach does this type of person need? A student in a big city is certainly more likely to feel addressed by a modern style of language and neologisms than a pensioner in a small village who may never even have heard of Anglicisms.

- **What exactly?** This question deals primarily with the content of the story, but above all with its central message: If you want to introduce your company or even the CEO, the narrator/hero and plot (the action) are naturally quite different than if you want to introduce a new product. Therefore, the *what is* very much related to the *why and* also to the *how,* similar to the Golden Circle. You should also ask yourself whether it is a one-off, rather unchanging story (founding story) - or recurring, perhaps even building on each other, narratives, for example the various stages of development of a new product, frequently asked customer queries or curious stories from everyday work life. No matter what you choose, there's one thing you must never forget: Your story should also add value to the audience! That's why it's also so important to describe conflict situations, even if this sounds paradoxical to many at first.

- **How? Above all, when and where?** Once you have decided which story(s) you want to tell, you must of course also consider how best to "get the word out". To answer this question in a meaningful way, you need to have defined your target audience precisely. Now it's a matter of identifying the media your audience uses. You also need to clarify whether a story should be published on a specific occasion (for example, on the company's 50th anniversary, at Christmas ...) or whether it could theoretically be published "at any time." An editorial plan can help you structure your thoughts, develop a longer-term strategy and play the appropriate media at the right time (see below).

- **Who is responsible for this?** Not only large companies should think about this point, but (especially) small and medium-sized companies as well as solo self-employed people. In large companies, for example, the entire marketing department could work on storytelling or just individual employees. Perhaps an extra position (often advertised as "content creator") is created precisely for this purpose. Or perhaps employees from other departments are integrated into the work process in phases (keyword: interdisciplinary teams). However, the task may also have to be outsourced and delegated to a text agency, for example. This could be the case, for example, if your company does not have sufficient personnel capacities or if you are self-employed and do not feel able to cope with the additional time required on your own. But even in this case, you need to answer all the preceding questions conscientiously, because otherwise even the best content creators in the world wouldn't be able to provide you with exactly what you need for your marketing. That's why I recommend you take matters into your own hands - after reading this guide, you'll finally be well equipped.

SMART Goals as a measure of success
So now that you've clarified the most important questions, let's turn our attention once again to the goal (or goals) you want to achieve with your marketing in general and your stories in particular. To clearly define this, the SMART Goal method is a good way to go:

S - Specific (specific)
M - Measurable
A - Attractive (i.e. "I am motivated to achieve this goal")
R - Realistic (realistic)
T - Timebound (time limited)

Essentially, this means that you think about what exactly you want to achieve, how and by when. This also makes it easier for you to break down larger projects or campaigns into smaller stages and subtasks.

A rather unfortunate formulated goal would be, for example: We want to increase our conversion rate (i.e. the rate of people who, for example, not only visit your website but also buy something in the web store).

Better: We want to increase our conversion rate by Y percent by time X. This concrete goal (based on your previous business figures) not only gives you a deadline and thus a time frame. The individual processes can also be measured objectively and progress can thus be monitored regularly. Something similar can also be formulated if you have determined in the course of your W-question analysis that it is time to open a new social media channel, for example.

5 ways to find ideas
After you have clarified which goals you are pursuing and who you want to address, it is now time to think about the concrete content. In most cases,

the founding story as well as stories about your employees, products and customer inquiries are suitable as initial starting points. Depending on how long your company has been around and how much is already known about you and your offering, the following tips can help you generate more ideas for your story(s).

1. Brainstorming - The classic
Brainstorming is about first collecting as many ideas as possible on a given topic. The ideas are evaluated later. Initially, anything is allowed, even supposedly "abstruse" ideas. As soon as no further input follows, the ideas are sorted (thematically) and examined for their feasibility. Often, this alone gives rise to further possibilities. In order to avoid a brainstorming session that is too extensive and inefficient, it is a good idea to set a time frame in which ideas can be expressed. Of course, there is the option to add ideas that pop up later.

2. Best practice analysis - What can you learn from already successful companies?

The term "imitation" certainly sounds rather negative at first, even more so when you actually just want to work out your uniqueness. However, the opposite is more likely to be the case, especially when it comes to a best-practice analysis. It is not about blindly copying (and in the worst case even word for word) what another company has already published. Rather, it's about taking inspiration from it. For example, if you're thinking about how to create an appealing "About Us" page, it's worth taking a look at other companies' websites. At best, you'll find clues as to what makes a successful page - and otherwise, you'll at least determine how NOT to do it. This is also a very important finding.

3. Back to the roots - How did you convince friends and relatives of your plans?

Sometimes you don't even have to look far afield to get (new) ideas, especially if you're self-employed or work in an SME. Why not ask friends and relatives what they associate with your business? This can be interesting for an "Among Us"

page as well as for stories around the values of y-
our company. Or even for so-called testimonials,
i.e. stories that are mostly told by customers (but
sometimes also by business partners). Maybe
funny anecdotes come to light that can be published well in a blog entry or in your social media
channels.

4. Use human capital creatively - Ask your
employees for suggestions
If you work in a larger company or generally like
to get your team more involved in the creative
process, it can be useful to put out a call to your
employees. For example, sales and customer service representatives may be able to provide you
with information about frequently asked questions or even the most curious ones. A supplier or
business partner may want to comment on what
it's like to work with you. A trainee or a new
employee might want to talk about how the company was received and whether there was an
obstacle or two right at the beginning that was finally solved through teamwork. As you can see,
there are endless possibilities.

5. Use calendar - Which (official) holidays and other occasions are relevant for you?

Another option is to consult the annual calendar and additionally Google and note any relevant holidays, commemorative days, festivals and other occasions that fit your company. For example, these could be days that are relevant to you from a historical or industry perspective. Or maybe you, your company or one of your employees is celebrating an anniversary? Maybe you are about to expand your product range or launch the successor to one of your bestsellers? Or maybe you just want to wish your customers a Merry Christmas or Easter?

This is only a small selection of methods for idea generation. Perhaps you can think of umpteen more. In any case, it is important that you think about the why and the who beforehand, so that you can weigh up which ideas are really purposeful. At this point, it should also be said once again that a story in marketing does not necessarily have to follow the classic 3- to 5-act structure of a drama - the type and length of a story result both from the topic/occasion of the same as well as from the parameters of the medium used: If you want to publish a blog post, you naturally have different options and technical requirements than if you "just want to send off a quick tweet", produce a radio spot or publish a photo series on Instagram about your latest product. (More on this in a moment when we talk about the editorial plan).

Now, when you start developing the ideas further, always check that your potential story has at least one character, one conflict, and its resolution ready. Of course, you can sometimes publish a story without these building blocks - for example, the Christmas greetings just mentioned. In general, however, you should - as already mentioned at the beginning - make sure that you offer your audience added value and also show yourself to be self-critical from time to time instead of writing 0815 gobbledygook or exaggerated self-praise. Nobody's perfect - and your customers know that too. Storytelling is not just about saying "We're here for you" or "You can rely on us," but about using concrete examples in emotional and image-rich stories to show customers how they can see that you actually live these values.

THE EDITORIAL PLAN - WELL PLANNED IS HALF WON

The goals and target group(s) have been defined, ideas have been collected ... then we can actually get started now, right? Not quite yet! In fact, good planning in storytelling is (at least) as important as writing the story itself. Especially when it comes to incorporating the individual stories into the overall marketing strategy.

So once you have clarified who you want to reach and why, you now need to determine where and how you want to publish your articles. To do this, you should first remind yourself of the most important characteristics of the various media - as well as the question of which media your target group uses and which you already use or still want to use. Once this question has been answered, you need to decide when to use which story and whether it should appear on several channels or just one. Because although it's generally true that "the mix makes the difference," not every story is suitable for every medium - and vice versa.

Selecting the right media - paying attention to special features

When it comes to choosing the right medium, two questions come to mind first: The first is the question of which channels you already use and which others you think could still suit your company. And second, which channels your target group uses. After all, the best blog is of little use to you if your target group is mainly on YouTube and Instagram. In addition to personal preferences, the possible reach of individual media and your financial resources also play a role in the choice of distribution media. For example, would you have the opportunity to run a nationwide TV spot? Or is it only enough for a small ad in a local newspaper? Do you want to spend any money at all on campaign placement? And what about financial resources for production in and of itself?

These questions are also crucial for choosing the right medium. In general, a distinction can be made between "Owned Media", "Paid Media" and "Earned Media". While "owned media" refers to your own channels (website, blog, Facebook, Twitter, Instagram, etc.), for the use of which you usually have no additional costs (except perhaps for the hosting of your domain), "paid media" refers to all media for the use of which you have to pay money (in the sense of placing ads). This can be, for example, ads in newspapers or on third-party websites, but also radio and TV spots. "Earned media, on the other hand, refers to all channels that give you publicity without your own intervention, through so-called word-of-mouth. This means that bloggers, for example, refer to your company or your products. Or perhaps a newspaper picks up the story of how you hosted a fundraiser this year to celebrate International XY Day. They are the opposite of "paid media," so to speak. Whereby these two categories are not to be confused with (active) influencer marketing, because that is something else entirely. However, it would go beyond the scope of this guide to go into this in more detail.

Regardless of the cost of the general types of media, they naturally also differ in how the content is presented. While websites and blogs are particularly suitable for longer texts and detailed stories, videos are shared on YouTube, and photography is predominantly used on Instagram and Pinterest to deliver the message(s) - even if, at least on Instagram, texts are increasingly making their way in. Twitter, on the other hand, is also predominantly text-based, but these may only contain a maximum of 280 characters (as of 2021). You should always keep this first brief overview of the different formats in mind when planning your stories. It's also worth creating an editorial plan to keep track of everything.

Why an editorial plan makes sense
While a private person can simply write, film, take pictures and share the results, a company should think about a strategy of what should be published where and when in order to ensure consistent communication and a common thread. This doesn't mean that Christmas greetings, for example, should be produced solely at the beginning of

December - of course, these can already be "pre-produced". But in any case, regardless of the production day of a story, it should be clear which overarching narrative thread your stories follow and in which order they will be presented to the outside world. As soon as several people are involved, an editorial plan is also the perfect tool to keep track not only of publication dates, but also of the entire creation and publication process. The key here is to create transparency and ensure that everyone involved knows who is responsible for which task and by when it must be completed.

In the editorial plan, it is not only noted which story is to appear when, but also on which channels. In this context, the responsibilities just mentioned as well as the required material (image, sound, text ...) and possibly also the production time and costs are noted. It is also helpful to indicate whether various media should refer to each other and to what extent adjustments are necessary from medium to medium.

Checklist: What belongs in the editorial plan
Ultimately, the editorial plan is something like an important cheat sheet: the more carefully it is

prepared, the smoother production and publication will run. It is usually easiest to set up the editorial plan as a table that can be expanded or broken down into more detail as required. For example, it can be an annual, quarterly, monthly, weekly Quarterly, monthly, weekly and daily overviews. This depends on your personal preferences, but also on the scope of your marketing activities. In general, the following information should be included in the editorial plan:

- **Planned release date** (+ alternative date, if applicable)
- **Theme/plot of the story**
- **Place/type of publication** (which channel, which format)
- **Specific requirements on the part of the medium** (presentation style, format)
- **Necessary production steps and resources** (e.g. video production)
- **Responsible person/department** (Are there also external stakeholders?)

If you can think of any other points that you think should be included in your editorial plan, be sure to add them - after all, the plan should make your life easier and therefore be tailored precisely to y-our needs. This checklist is primarily intended to give you a first impression of what needs to be thought of in any case before you can finally get started with the actual storytelling.

IMPLEMENTATION - GETTING INTO WRITING

Congratulations, you now have almost all of your preparations in place and can get down to writing. To make sure you don't get bogged down in the middle of your story, you should first get all the tools you need, briefly check that you have clarified the most important questions and have the building blocks for the story ready. And then it's a matter of: Practice, practice, practice, because as we all know, no master has ever fallen from the sky.

You should always have these tools at hand
Not only during the actual writing process, but it's best to always and everywhere have a notebook and pen with you - even if you prefer to record everything digitally. Double is better than double,

and it would be a real shame if you forgot your best idea again because you didn't have a chance to take notes at the time you came up with it.

The same is also true for the notes that have already been taken on your story. You should keep them all in the same place, whether it's a loose-leaf collection or an electronic document (or several). These notes don't have to be in order yet, that will follow in a second step - especially since you may want or need to change the order you originally planned.

You should also keep your editorial plan in sight, or at least handy at all times. This strengthens your focus and also helps you always keep in mind for which channel(s) you are preparing a story.

Also, feel free to put books at your desk that contain stories that have captivated you yourself. This can serve as inspiration and motivation, both in terms of content and language, when you get stuck. Also useful are a dictionary and a synonym dictionary to have support especially on the linguistic level. And, of course, this guidebook, so that you can read up on the best way to proceed at any time.

The red thread - organize notes and structure plot

So now that you have all the important questions answered and all the tools in place, you can finally turn your attention to your story. Take another look at your notes and check them as you go:

- Do I have (at least) one character, the hero?

- Is there a conflict?

- Do I have a solution ready?

- Do I know why, for whom and for which channel I am producing the story?

- Do I already know roughly how the plot should play out?

If you can answer yes to the first four questions, you are ready to go into medias res. Otherwise, I recommend that you take your time to review the previous chapters of the guide and critically comparc your current notes with the analysis questions.

The fifth question, on the other hand, is more about whether you are an "intuitive writer" or a "planner". Both are good; often these two types differ mainly in the experience they have already gained. While intuitive writers, after the aforementioned preliminary work, actually already have their narrative in mind and only need to put it down on paper, planning writers feel the need to organize their notes and first roughly sketch out the plot (i.e., the course of the action) before they feed their story with content and life.

If you are an intuitive writer - great! Then you can go right ahead and write down a first draft of your story. Once you're broadly satisfied, you can basically skip ahead to the "Before Publication" chapter if you'd like. If you're trying your hand at storytelling for the first time or are a planning writer, I recommend that you also read the following subchapters carefully before you finally get down to writing. There you'll find, among other things, more tips and information on building a story and choosing the right language/narrative style.

The structure of your story
Generally speaking, your story will need an introduction, a body, and a conclusion, much like your previous school essays. However, depending on the format you choose and the occasion, the specific structure may differ. In more classic stories, the relevant W questions are first answered at the beginning, a so-called setting is presented. You learn who the hero is and what he usually does. Then the conflict begins to unfold. This conflict and the search for its resolution form the main part of your story. And finally, the resolution follows at the end. Such a structure is interesting, for example, if you want to tell the founding story, or if you are introducing a new product (see above, keyword: Apple).

However, it can often be advantageous to twist the structure a bit in order to attract more attention and thus more interest. For example, you could use the introduction to give the audience a brief preview of what to expect in the story - without giving away the ending, of course. You'll often find this method in tabloid and celebrity news stories when the opening sentence is, for example, "She's done it again!"

In this context, the so-called "kitchen call" was invented, which gives the answer to this question and is usually also understood as the main message of the text. The kitchen call is a sentence that clarifies the most important W-questions, for example, the sentence you would also use if you had to pack your story into a single tweet. The phrase "kitchen call" goes back to Henry Nannen, who understood it to be the sentence a man "calls into the kitchen" to his wife while reading the newspaper to succinctly summarize the article he just read - for example, "Gee, the government wants more taxes again." The sentence is informative enough to explain what it is about (tax increase), but does not yet clarify why or what taxes are involved. This encourages the reader to read the rest of the article.

As you can see, your story does not necessarily have to follow the structure of a drama, especially depending on the topic and the chosen channel. Nevertheless, it is worthwhile to follow it a bit and ask yourself what information your addressee needs in any case. After all, this information should not appear only at the end of the story - at least not without having been teased beforehand by an appropriate arc of suspense.

When choosing the structure, be guided primarily by the questions "Who do I want to reach with this?" - a professional audience, for example, has different prior knowledge and expectations than a potential new customer - and "In which channel and in which format will my story be published?" Because although you should ideally dictate (at least roughly) the story to be told even with videos, you naturally have very different design options with image and film formats than with a pure text format.

The tone makes the music - the choice of narrative style

So if you now know WHAT you want to tell, you now have to decide for yourself HOW you want to tell it. Again, you need to know who you are addressing, through what channel, and for what reason. You see: If you've done your homework well, the actual writing process will be much easier for you right away, because you can't avoid the W-questions. You certainly had a similar experience when you founded your company and started thinking about strategic (marketing) issues.

You or you?

A fundamental question when addressing your audience is whether you should address them by their first name or by their first name. On the one hand, this depends on the nature of your company (a young tech start-up will address its customers differently than a luxury fashion label) and on the other hand, once again, on the target group itself and the chosen medium. For example, if you want to acquire new young customers via Instagram, YouTube and the like, the "you" is much more appropriate than the "you". Conversely, potential new investors or members of your board may be less enthusiastic if you don't address them by their first name. In any case, however, you should prefer a direct address (you/they) to an indirect one (man). That's how you build a bond. And as you've already learned, that's one of the most important factors in storytelling in marketing.

Formal or "young and modern"?

Here, too, the topic, target group and format are crucial. If you are presenting your company as a future employer for trainees and it fits your industry and your corporate values, there is nothing to stop you from loosening up old stiff patterns a bit and maybe even writing in a bit of everyday language. But please don't use too much supposedly current youth language. Because this changes at such a pace that you would probably have to completely revise your career page at least once a year in order to stay up-to-date. Either way, it is important that you use understandable and correct German. Otherwise, everything will quickly come across as unprofessional, no matter how great your stories actually are. Formal stories are especially useful if you're presenting the latest studies on your industry, you're addressing an expert audience, or it's simply still the custom in your field - for example, in insurance.

What about humor, irony and sarcasm?

In principle, it is also possible to tell a story with a wink - especially if, for example, it is about a conflict being solved by chance or with the help of a curious idea. Or when a supposedly major (technical) problem was solved with a small twist of the wrist. However, the dosage is important. If you frequently share rather humorous stories, this could lead to you being taken less seriously - when you were at school, who would have been more likely to believe that lessons were cancelled because the teacher was ill: the break-time clown or the class representative? While self-mockery is fine now and then to remain authentic and convey that you know that not everything always goes like clockwork for you either, you should definitely refrain from sarcastic remarks on a corporate level! This can quickly backfire and make you seem unsympathetic or even insensitive. If, for example, you pick up on a curious customer or employee story and you want to tell it with a little wink, you must also make sure that the person in question is not clearly identifiable - after all, no one should be exposed. (Not only because a juicy legal dispute could threaten ...).

The use of technical and foreign words

In most cases, less is more. And if you can do without complex word and sentence constructions altogether, it's even better. The point is to evoke emotions.

However, incomprehensible texts and "technical jargon" are most likely to lead to defensive reactions instead of positive emotions, if at all. The human brain can process information best when it is presented with it in the form of images and familiar patterns. Abstract concepts, on the other hand, are difficult or impossible to process. If you want to read more about this, I can recommend Daniel Kahneman's "Fast Thinking, Slow Thinking".

In concrete terms, this means for you: If you want or need to restructure, expand or change personnel in your company, for example, then don't talk about "change management", "reallocation of resources" or similar complicated-sounding processes. Instead, describe pictorially that it is necessary, for example, to close department X because Y. Or that you are currently planning a change in your company. Or that you are planning to open a branch in another city because it has become apparent that the demand for your products/services is particularly high (there). Or that you're going to create a new position in your marketing department so that someone can take care of storytelling in the future. One of the few exceptions where the use of foreign and technical words is explicitly encouraged is if you are submitting an article to the trade press or giving a relevant presentation at an industry event/to a professional audience. However, this also results from the designation of the corresponding addressees.

Practice makes perfect - more tips and tricks
As you've no doubt already noticed, the list of things you should absolutely do (or absolutely avoid doing) could go on forever. But no matter how long the list would ultimately be, it would never be complete. And you (and everyone else, including me) would still make a few mistakes, especially at the beginning - after all, no master has ever fallen from the sky. On the contrary, various studies have shown that people need to have practiced a new skill for an average of about 10,000 hours to actually acquire a corresponding masterful qualification in it. So there's only one thing to

do: practice, practice, practice; be willing to learn from your mistakes, and above all, don't get discouraged. Now here are a few more general tips that can help you make your story even better.

No nested sentences!
To help your audience follow your story, keep it as simple as possible - linguistically speaking. Long sentence structures consisting of several main and subordinate clauses make your text more complicated than it needs to be. This can quickly become "too much trouble" for the reader. Sometimes, however, tapeworm sentences also give the impression that the author himself does not really know what he actually wanted to say. Not a pleasant idea! Therefore: Keep it short and simple (KISS). For example, try to use as few sentence structures as possible. Make two (or three) short sentences out of one long one. You will learn more about simplicity in the following chapter.

Pictures, pictures and more pictures
Images arouse emotions. And associations. And that doesn't just mean images in the sense of photos and videos, but above all the proverbial

"pictures in the head. That's why in the American-speaking world - even if it seems confusing at first glance - people often talk about "show, don't tell" when it comes to good storytelling. There are two things behind this: On the one hand, it is a matter of not only proclaiming (abstract) values such as "reliability," "quality," and "customer orientation," but also of emphasizing them through concrete examples. And secondly, closely related to this and already briefly mentioned above: It's about "picking up the audience where they stand." This means that you create concrete images in the minds of your addressees - because this also activates the associated associations and emotions that ultimately ensure that your company is also linked with these characteristics. Your story must therefore be told in such a pictorial way that the reader has the feeling of experiencing it for themselves. The better you succeed in creating images, the longer your story will stick in the memory of your addressee.

Adjectives in moderation, not in masses

Nowadays, however, it has become common for many people to want to achieve the figurativeness of their narrative primarily through the increased use of adjectives - often, however, these are rather superfluous and artificially puff up the story instead of offering added value. A classic example of this is "terrible catastrophes" (after all, the very definition of the word indicates that it is seldom something harmless and basically nothing good). Similarly, pleonasms à la "white horse" and "black raven". Doubles like "enormous damage" (or the use of the word "enormous" in general) should also be avoided. Again, as with foreign words: Less is more.

The eternal suffering with superlatives
It's not just adjectives that are often overused - it's also the use of superlatives. If, for example, you praise every one of your products as "the best" (or worse: as "the absolute best"), the desired effect is quickly lost or can even turn into the opposite: If you constantly speak of yourself only in the very highest terms and never show any self-criticism, you may be a bit too self-absorbed and thus potentially out of touch with reality - not a quality you want in a service provider, supplier or cooperation partner. Apart from that, the constant use of su-perlatives (even more so when they don't exist in

such a way, such as "the only one" instead of "the only one") comes across rather like a kind of permanent advertising show. This has nothing to do with good marketing in general, nor with stylish storytelling in particular. That's why you're welcome to practice modesty here: not everything has to be touted as "super mega great" in order to be perceived as such by customers.

So much for the tips and tricks. Now it's time for you to get to work and practice, practice, practice. Once you've written your story and feel the need to publish it right now, it's time to take a short break.

Take another deep breath before you turn your attention to the penultimate chapter (and thus also the last major proactive step). And above all, be proud of yourself! If you've made it this far, you've already done most of the work.

BEFORE PUBLICATION

Done! You have successfully analyzed what stories you want to tell. You know why you are doing it and when, where and how the story should be published. You have finished writing the story and now only one thing is missing: the publication. But wait! Before you rush to press the appropriate release buttons, you should thoroughly check your story yourself and/or have it checked - especially in terms of content and linguistic design.

Check content with AIDA and KISS
You've probably heard of the AIDA formula and the KISS principle in your career. These two methods are excellent for checking the content of your story once again for relevance and comprehensibility.

A - Attention: The introduction to your narrative must attract attention (e.g. the title).
I - Interest: You must arouse interest in the subject/company/product
D - Desire: The addressee should develop a positive emotional connection (and, for example, a desire to buy).

A - Action: you encourage the addressee to act (for example, to buy your products)

Although the AIDA formula is oriented more towards classic marketing and advertising strategies, you can still use it to at least check whether your story is told in a "captivating" way and makes the audience want to follow it attentively to the end. The basic idea of the AIDA formula can be integrated especially well in stories about your products or services, but also in testimonials from your employees or former customers and business partners. However, it is not necessarily suitable for optimizing your corporate story, although it also benefits from lively storytelling. In any case, the KISS principle is a good way to ensure that your stories are easy to understand and free of unnecessary frills.

KISS stands for **"Keep It** Short **(and) Simple"**. Short refers primarily to the fact that you should avoid superfluous information, words and phrases. Check that the plot follows a common thread and doesn't get too lost in details and subplots. Eliminate duplications and other unnecessary words, as mentioned above in the tips-and-tricks section. This will also automatically make your story easier to understand and your core message will be clear. Keeping the story simple means, first and foremost, that you should keep both the narrative structure simple and straightforward (for example, by telling a story chronologically or structuring it with subheadings) and the linguistic design. Base your story on the expected prior knowledge of your target audience. And then take it down another notch. Use short, clear sentences. Use figurative language that activates the reader's imagination. Use concrete examples, but don't go into too much detail - if it turns out afterwards that exactly this (missing) detail is of particular interest to the audience, you've automatically found another story to tell.

Four-eyes principle in proofreading
It's not just the structure and content of your narrative that you should scrutinize again before publishing. Linguistic correctness is just as important. That's why your text should be carefully checked again for possible errors in spelling, grammar, syntax (sentence structure) and punctuation -

preferably by at least one other person who has not yet read the text. Because you probably know this from other texts: At some point, you've read them so many times that you literally can't see the mistakes anymore. Even if, for example, entire words are missing, you no longer notice this after a certain point - because you know the text inside out and your brain therefore automatically reads it correctly. Don't worry, this is not unique to you! That's why I recommend that you hand over the proofreading, i.e. the linguistic checking of your text, to someone else. After all, four eyes see more than two. And on top of that, you'll get initial feedback on how (well) your story is actually received. You should definitely ask for this feedback, after all, it will help you to become even better at storytelling in the future.

Final check: Does the story fit the chosen medium?

Now that you've put your story through its paces once again, it's time to take another critical look at one last point: Have you also adapted your story to the specific requirements of your chosen medium? To put it exaggeratedly: The best five-page story is of little use to you if you were actually supposed to send a short tweet. Just as little as you should be able to come up with a short, flippant "Even the best make mistakes" slogan during a presentation for new investors. These are two extreme examples, and even a complete storytelling beginner knows that these two examples are absolute no-goes and probably rarely occur in practice.

Nevertheless, it often happens that marketing campaigns do not pay sufficient attention to the specifics of the individual channels. Especially when a campaign is to be published across several platforms, this last control instance is often neglected. Then it's "Oh, we'll just take a few sentences from our blog post and use them for Twitter" or "We'll quickly take a photo for Instagram and tell people to read up on our blog for more info". This method actually leads to success in very few cases. That's because the way users interact with each other on the various platforms alone is very diverse. This is also due in large part to the users themselves; age and social status in particular have a major influence on the (non-)choice of a particular medium on the one hand and the chosen communication style on the other.

The reverse is also true for you: A channel that is primarily based on image or video contributions opens up completely different possibilities for you (especially in terms of the "setting") than a purely text-based publishing portal. At this point, you can once again see how important it is not to just write wildly and publish the first idea that comes to mind. It is more effective to collect your thoughts, organize them, plan the individual editing processes ... and then implement them step by step. When you have finished and checked your story, you have done it.

Now you are done with everything and can finally press the "Publish" button with pride - congratulations!

AFTER PUBLICATION: MONITORING AND SUCCESS ANALYSIS OF YOUR CONTRIBUTIONS

Although you've more than earned another short breather, you're still not completely off the hook after publishing your post: In order to implement storytelling successfully and permanently into your marketing strategy, you must of course also subject it to constant success monitoring. Remember your SMART goal: What do you want to achieve with your stories? Admittedly, it would go beyond the scope of this guide to discuss all the analytics tools in detail. That being said, I imagine you already have a good sense of what matters in the course of your previous marketing activities. Basically, though, here are a few more ways you can monitor the success of your stories:

On the one hand, you can use the so-called "Insights" on platforms such as Facebook, Instagram and Co. These are provided by the platform and allow you to find out, for example, how many people interact with your post and in what way they did so.

If the information provided by the respective platform itself is not sufficient, there are also so-called (often fee-based) third-party providers (such as Google Analytics), which can make further data and its analysis available to you. When using them, however, pay attention to the terms and conditions of the platform you are using (some threaten to block your user account if you use third-party providers) and, above all, make sure that you do not violate the European Data

Protection Regulation (GDPR). The same also applies if, for example, you install analytics tools and plugins on your website and blog. In this case, caution is the mother of china: Put up a clearly visible notice about what data you collect and for what purpose - the so-called cookie notice. It's best to allow website visitors to decide for themselves which data may be stored and used. This will save you a lot of potential litigation. Surely you've seen such cookie permission requests yourself many times when you've been on the Internet.

Another option would be to conduct surveys or have them conducted. However, nowadays this variant of gaining knowledge is rather difficult and is often linked to the use of large financial, personnel and time resources. Alternatively, you can carry out so-called A-/B-Testings. In this case, part of your target group is shown version A of your contribution - and the other part gets to see a modified B version. In this way, it is tested in relation to a specific factor X in which way it is better received by the target group.

In conclusion, we can state the following on the subject of monitoring and success analysis: Similar to the creation of the post, it is also true here that a reasonable preliminary work is already half the battle. The more precisely you define the goal of your campaign/post beforehand, the easier it is for you to determine the factors to be analyzed. And the more precisely you know what the respective success factors are, the better you can equip yourself to monitor and analyze them. This, in turn, will allow you to better tailor future stories to your target audience and the channels you use. It is therefore very important that you also regularly update your editorial plan and storytelling style and incorporate the new insights you gain. Because by doing so, you make storytelling your marketing advantage in the market!

So that in the future, as soon as you feel confident enough, you no longer have to work through the entire guide line by line, you will find an 11-point plan on the following pages that once again shows you the most important steps. This way you can continue to comfortably plan your story from start to finish and become a professional storyteller yourself. I wish you lots of fun and success in the process!

Short and sweet: 11 steps to storytelling in marketing

To summarize the contents of the guide once again, you will find an 11-point quick guide below to help you get your story right from start to finish and then get it out there. Of course, you are welcome to expand it with your own experiences and insights.

1. Define your goal and answer the W-questions
Remember the "Golden Circle": WHY do you do what you do? HOW do you do it? And WHAT exactly are you doing? Answering these questions will already give you a sense of where you are headed. Also, clarify: WHO do I want to reach? WHY do I want to address this target group? HOW, WHERE and WHEN do I want to reach them? WHO is responsible for the implementation? Also important: HOW HIGH is my budget?

2. Collect ideas that fit your goals
General ideas: Founding story, stories about products, new trends and studies in the industry, employee and customer stories, stories about trade shows and events attended. In addition, brainstorming and best practice analyses are suitable for generating further ideas.

3. Plan your posts and create an editorial plan
Think about an overall strategy and record it in an editorial plan. This should include which story is to be published when and where. You should also note how much lead time you need and whether, for example, external service providers (such as

video producers) need to be brought on board or additional material needs to be procured.

4. Have ready all the tools you may need
In case of doubt, these are at least your notes and this guidebook. As a further aid, anything that promotes your writing flow and at the same time ensures that you do not lose focus is suitable.

5. Outline the plot
Who is the hero of the story? From which perspective is the story told? What is the initial situation? What conflict is it about? Are there other characters? How is the conflict finally resolved?

6. Get started
Let off steam, have fun. Practice makes perfect and the more you try, the more likely you are to find the style that suits you.

7. AIDA, KISS and the question of the right structure
Once you're happy with your story and feel the impulse to publish it directly, take the time to put it through its paces. Make sure your sentences are

short and concise. Make sure that superfluous plot lines, platitudes and filler words are cut from the text - your audience will thank you. Also check again whether you have used figurative, emotionalizing language and avoided technical and foreign words as far as possible.

8. Have the story proofread again
Once you have checked your story, have at least one other person (a colleague/staff member or a professional editor) check it for linguistic errors or other inconsistencies. Spelling and grammar in particular, but also sentence structure and punctuation should be closely scrutinized. The rule here is: four eyes see more than two (and six eyes see more than four ...).

9. Check again if the story is adapted to the desired medium
Finally, ask yourself once again whether your narrative is not only adapted to the desired target group, but also to the selected medium. Recall once again the particularities of each platform and check whether you have taken them into account. For example, a tweet may be no longer than 280

characters, while a blog post could well be 1,000 words or more.

10. Publish the story at the scheduled time
You don't have to write your story "when you need it". The advantage of the editorial plan and content marketing/storytelling in general is that you can simply write the story when it suits you - even months before the planned publication date. Just make a note in your editorial plan and press the button at the appropriate time.

11. Check the effectiveness of your stories
Use analytics tools to see which stories are resonating well. Adjust your editorial plan and storytelling style accordingly on an ongoing basis.